MW00872595

MONSTER TRUCK

COLORING BOOK FOR KIDS

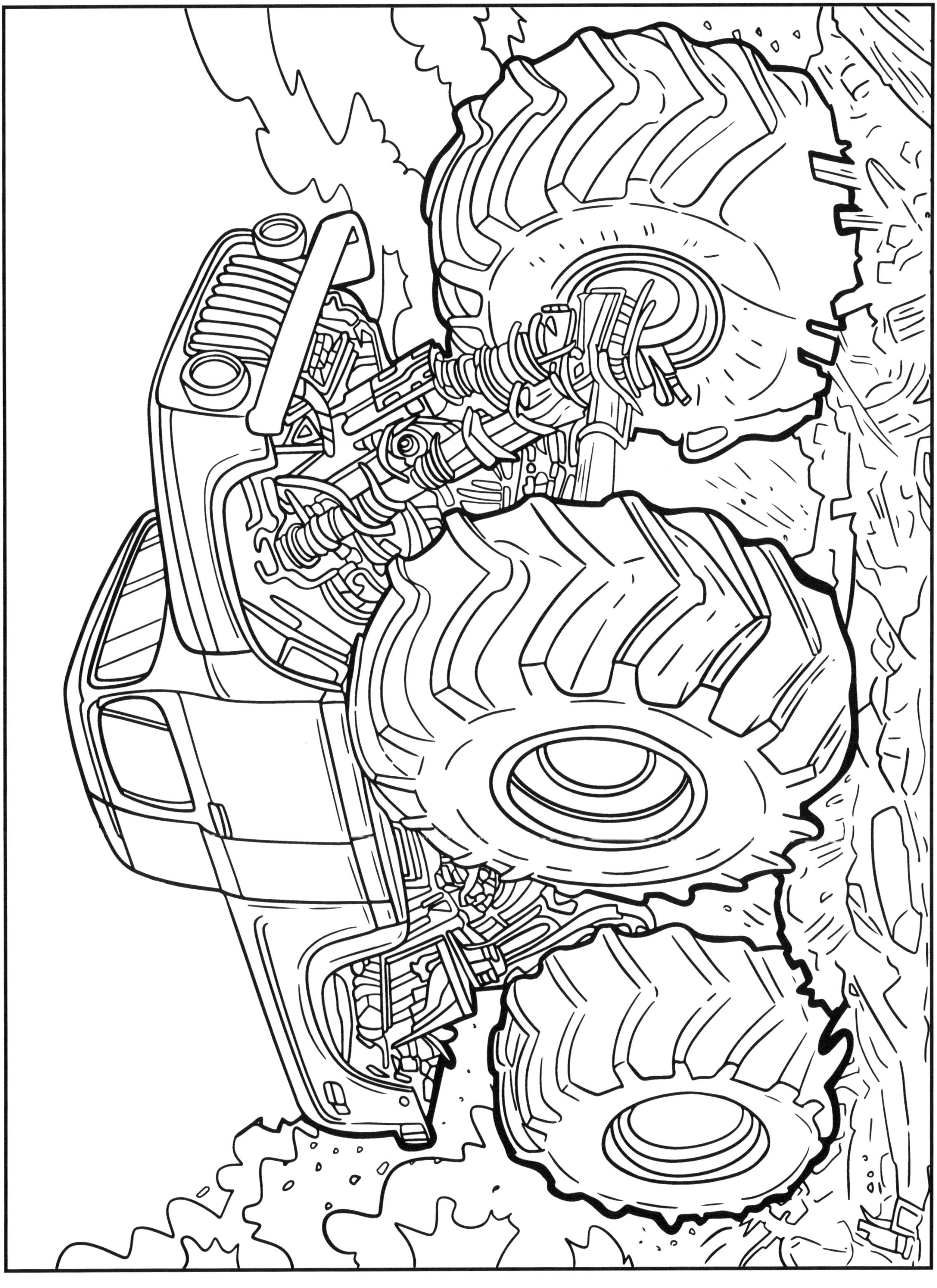

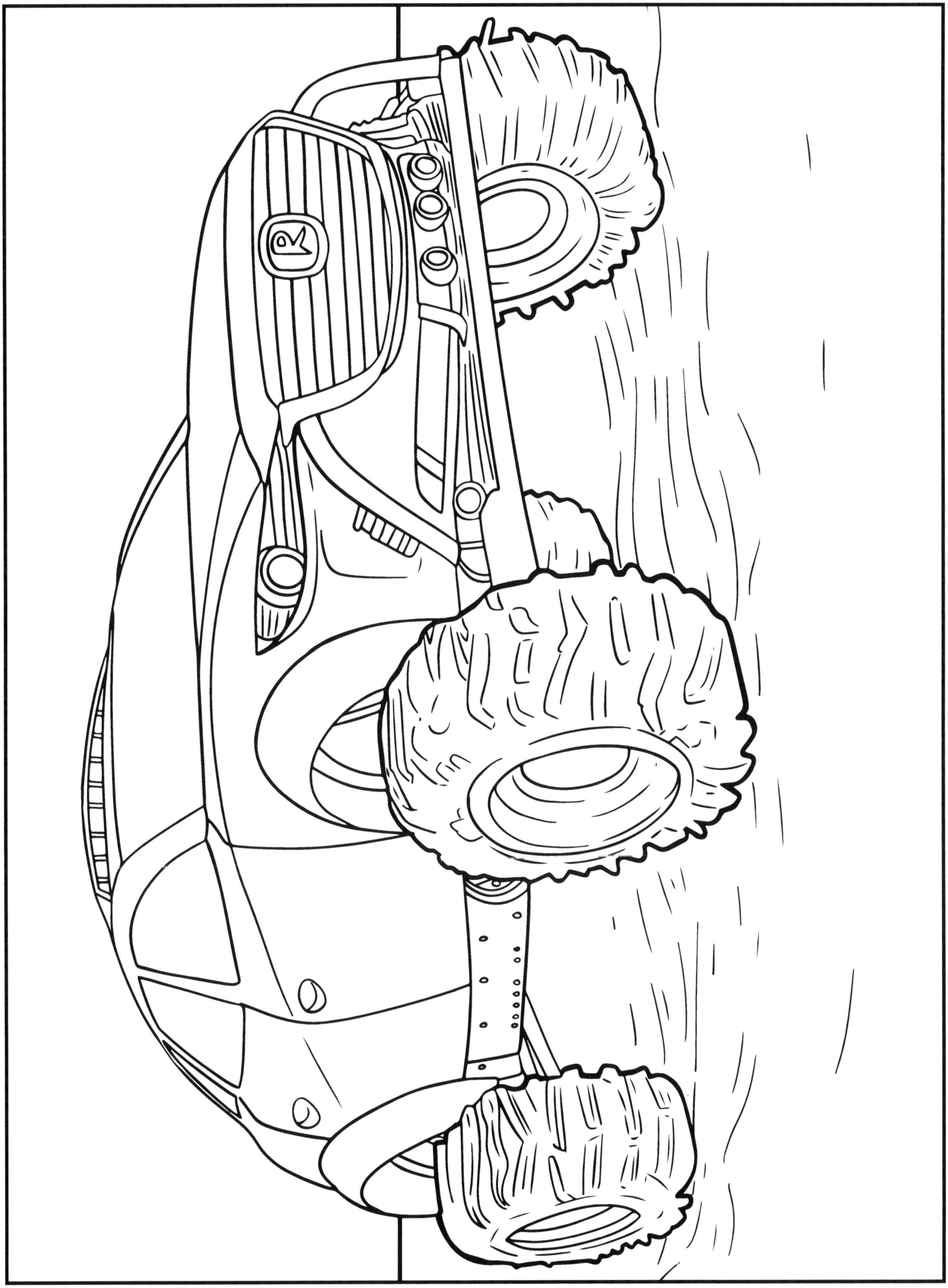

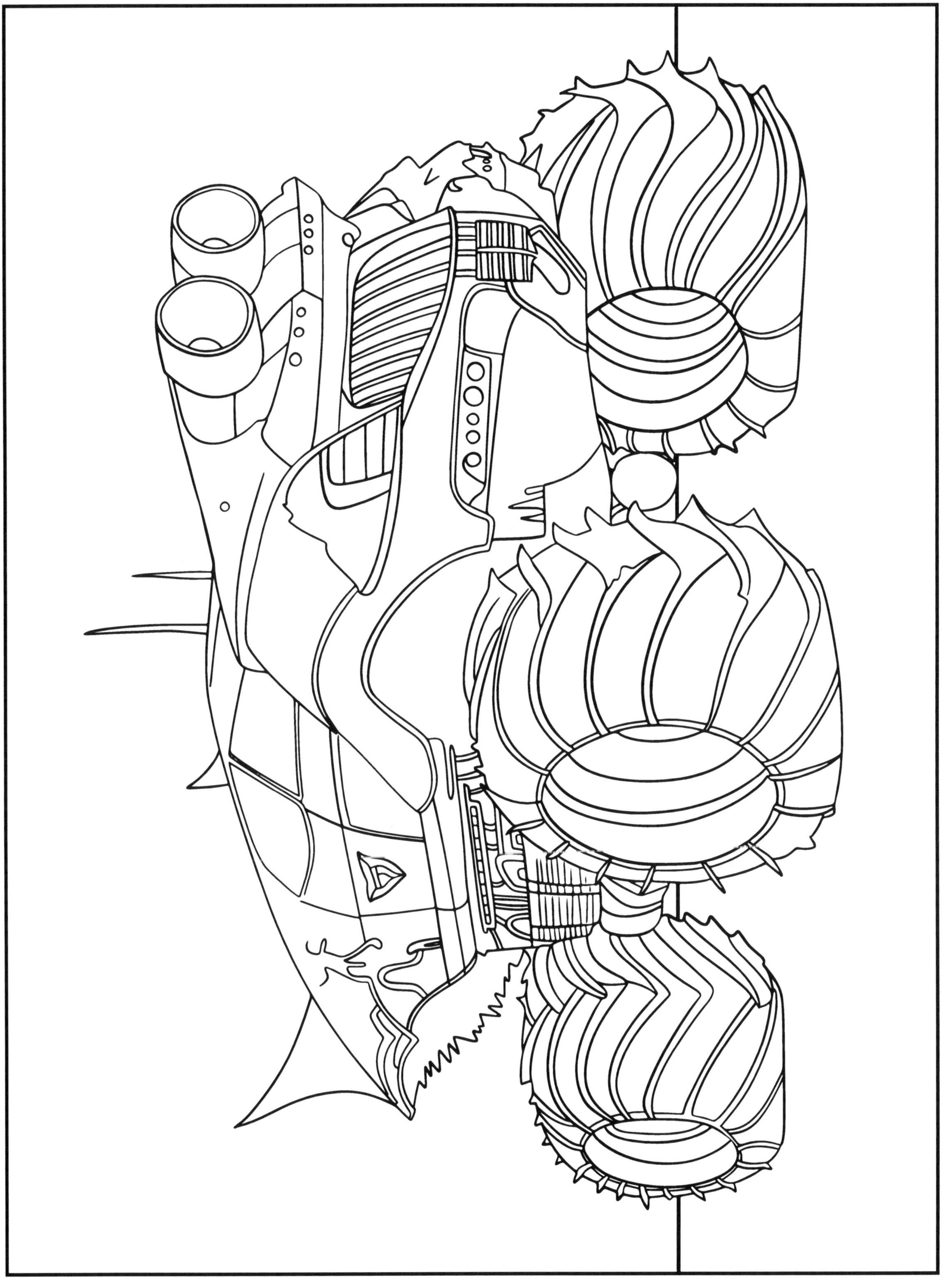

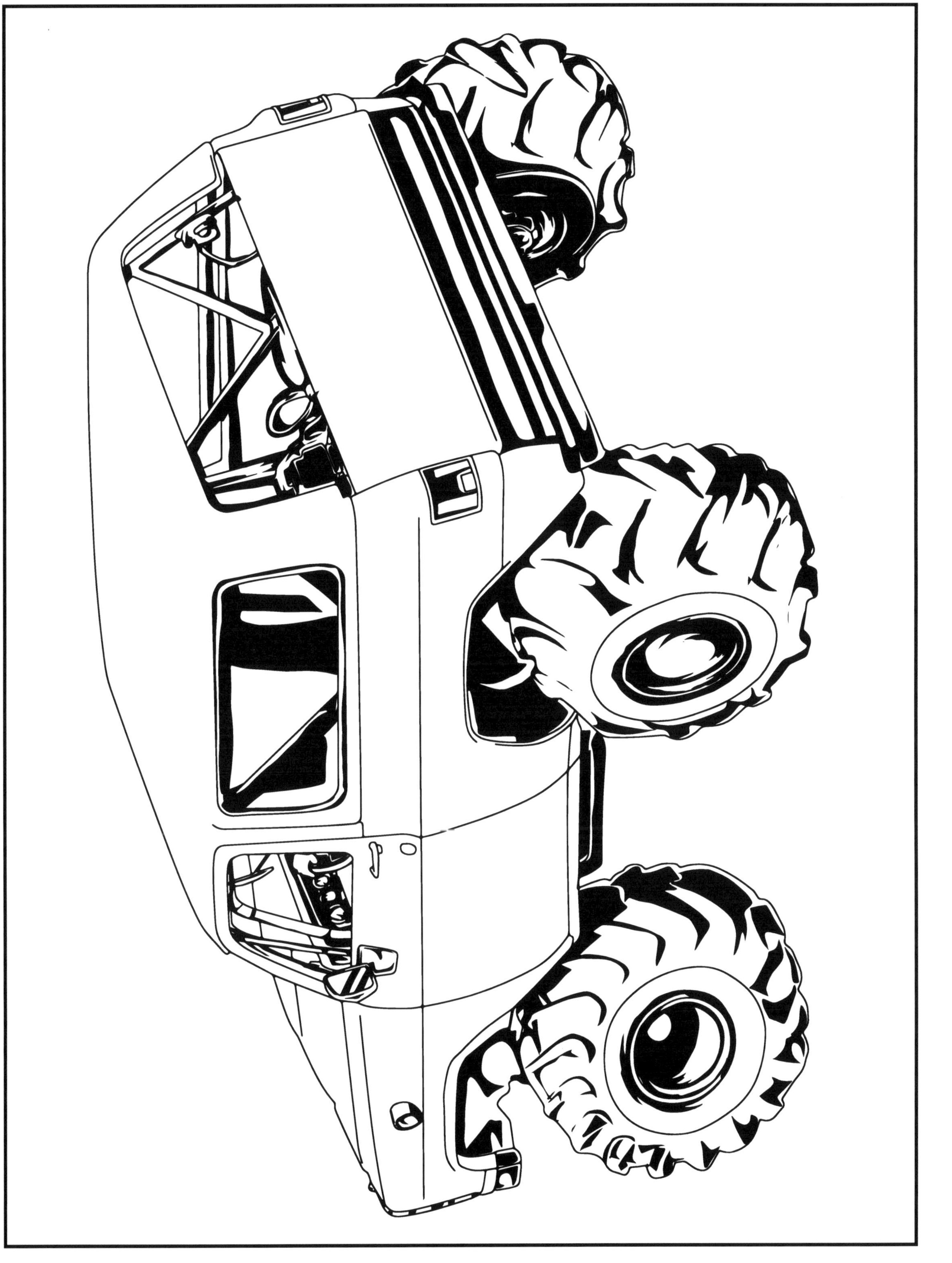

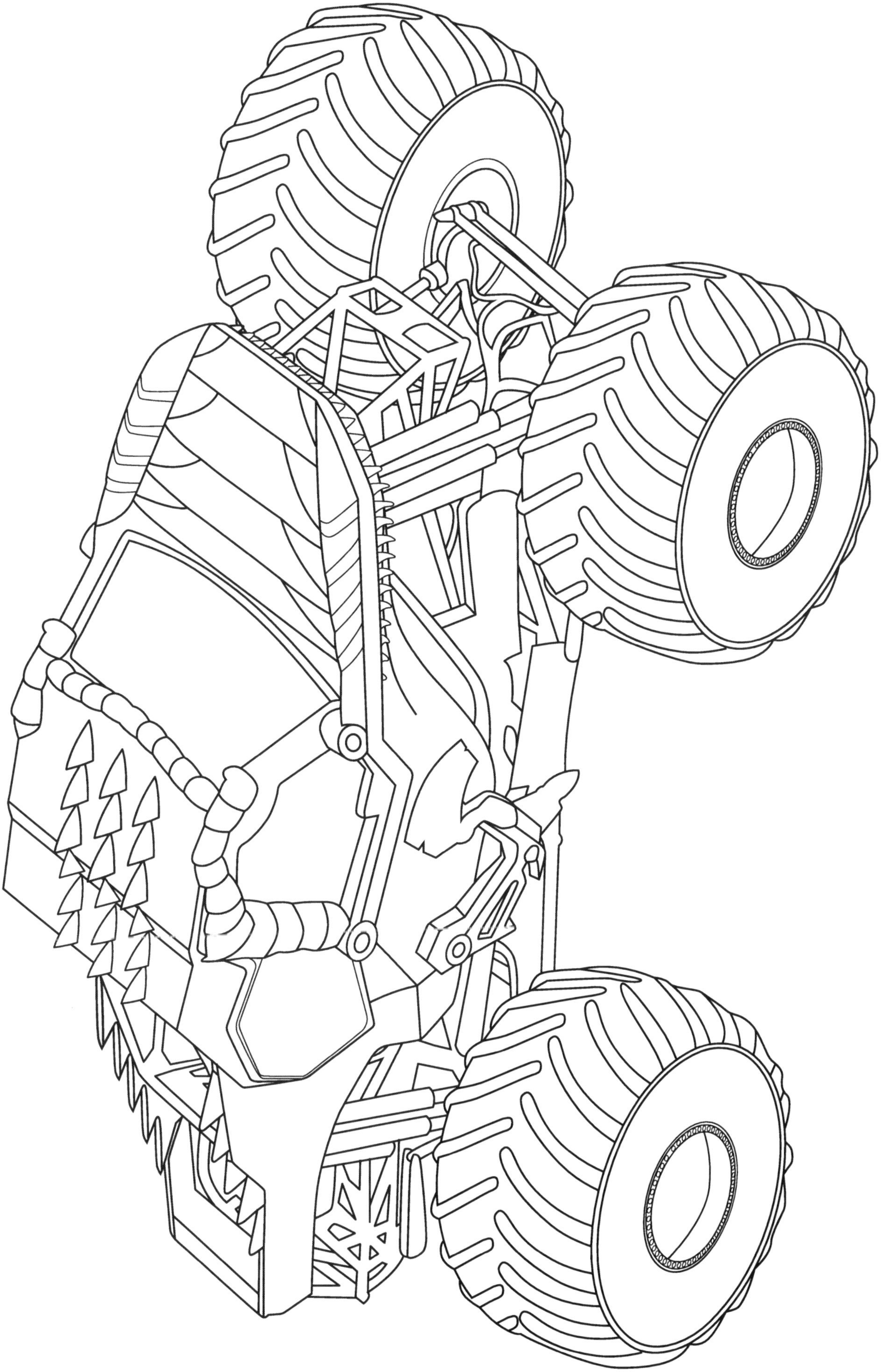

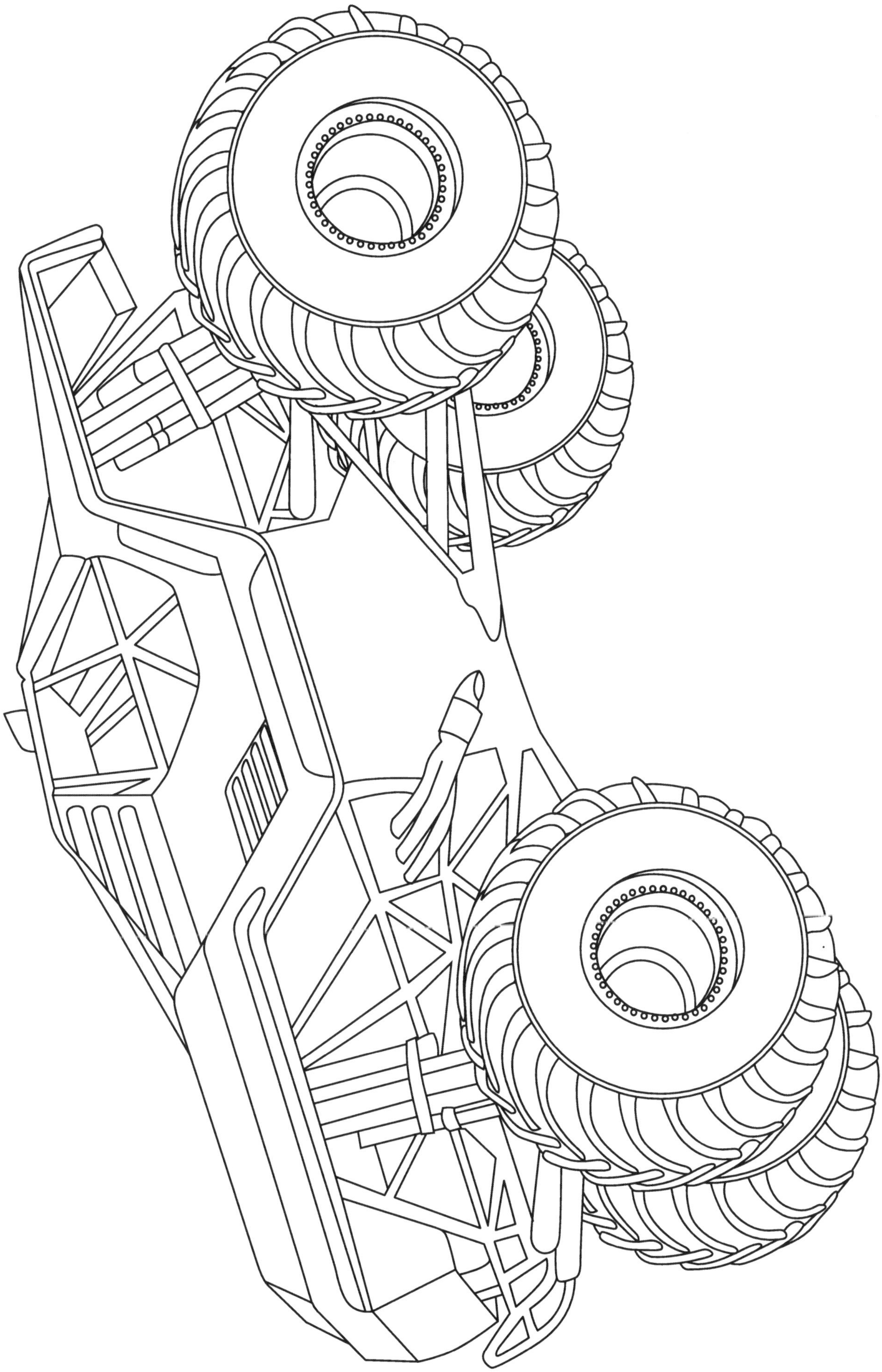

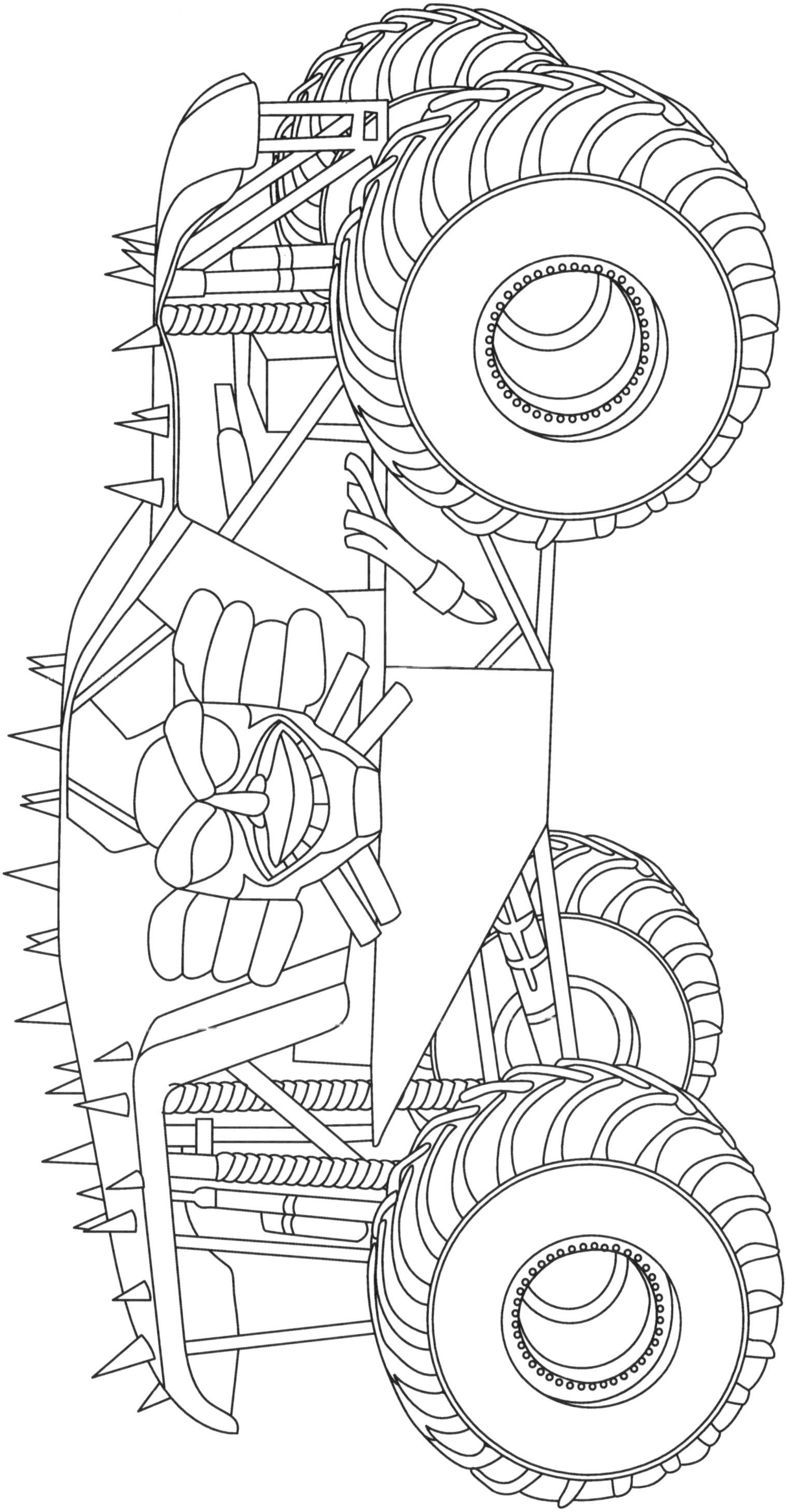

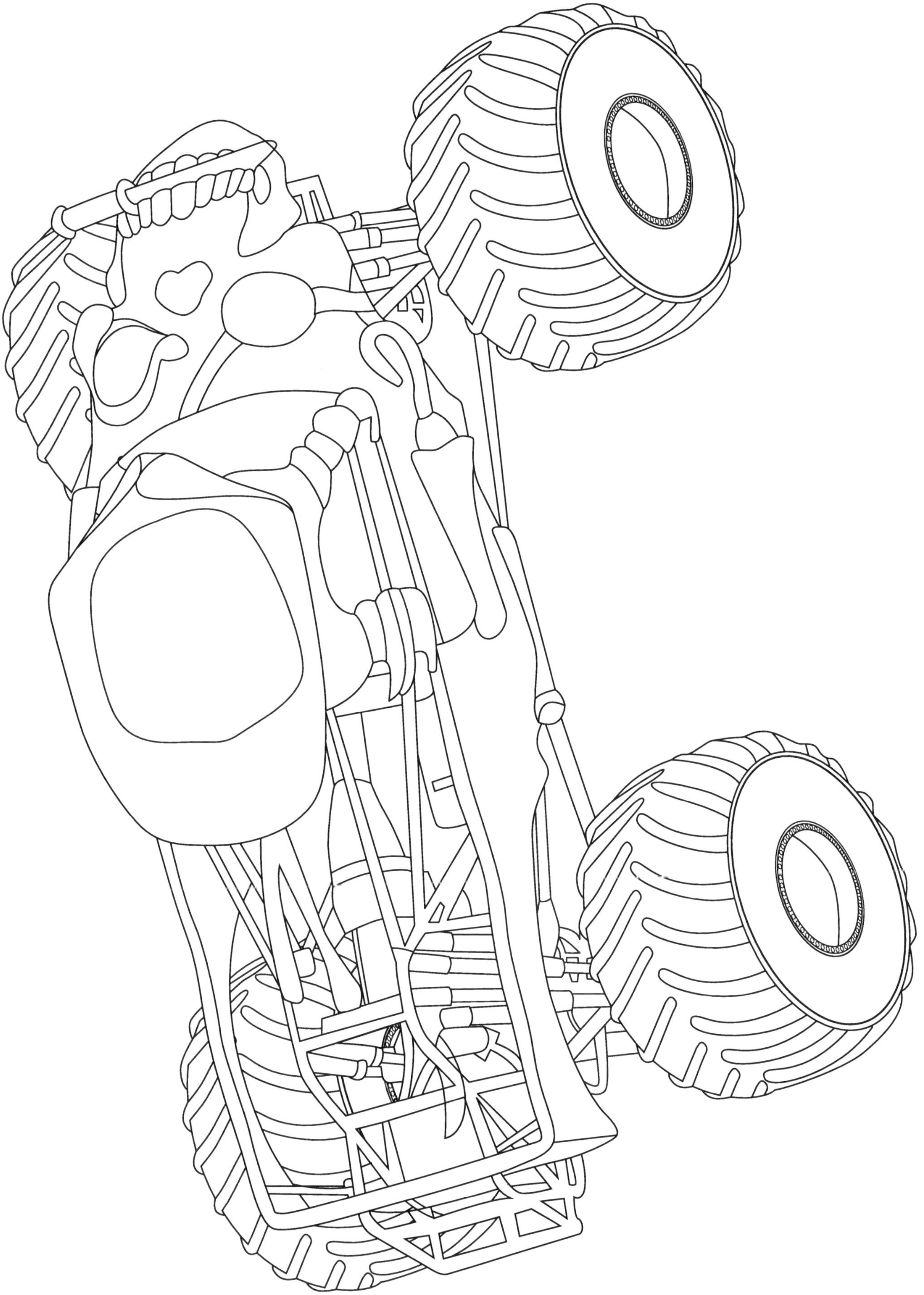

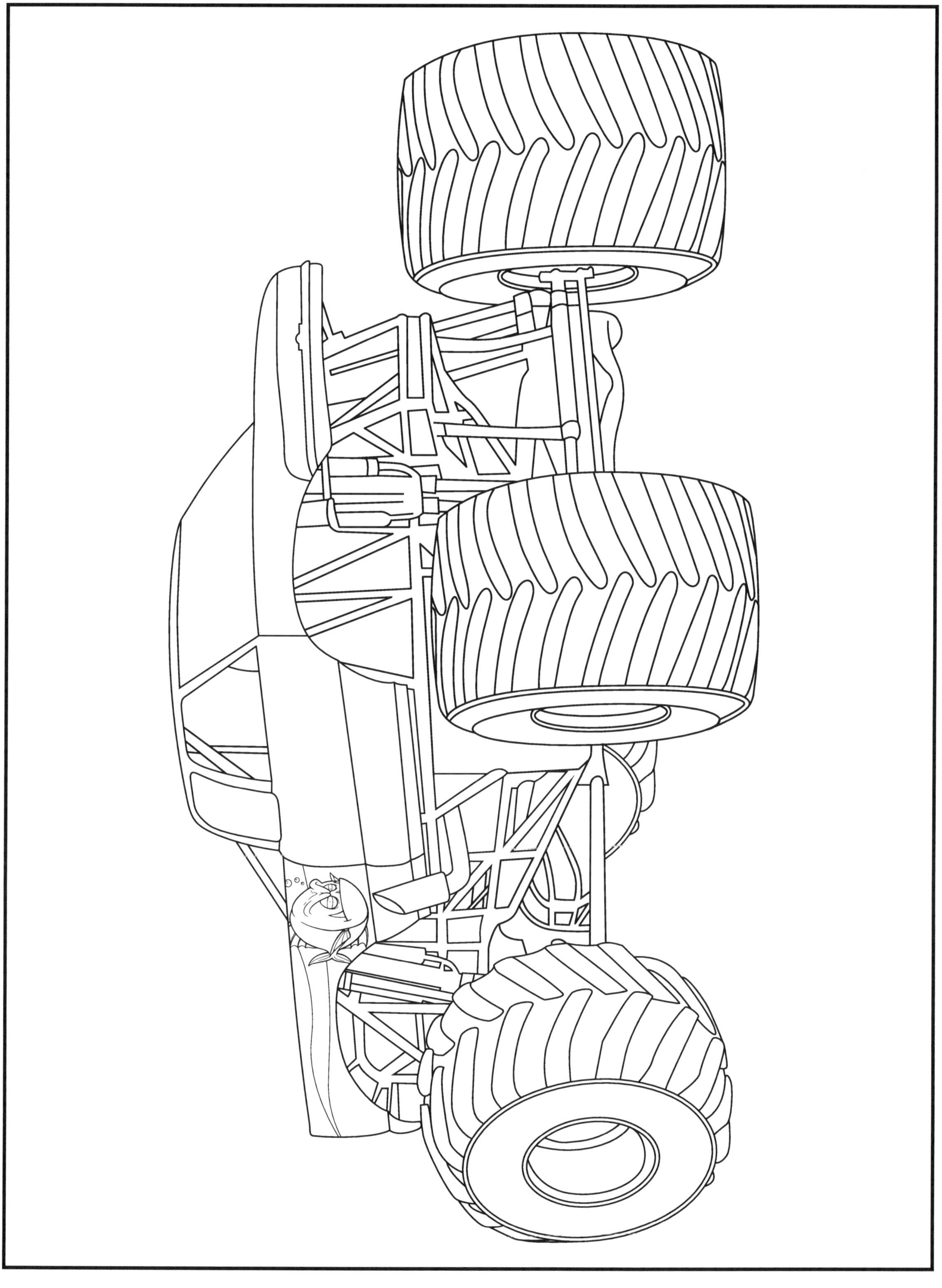

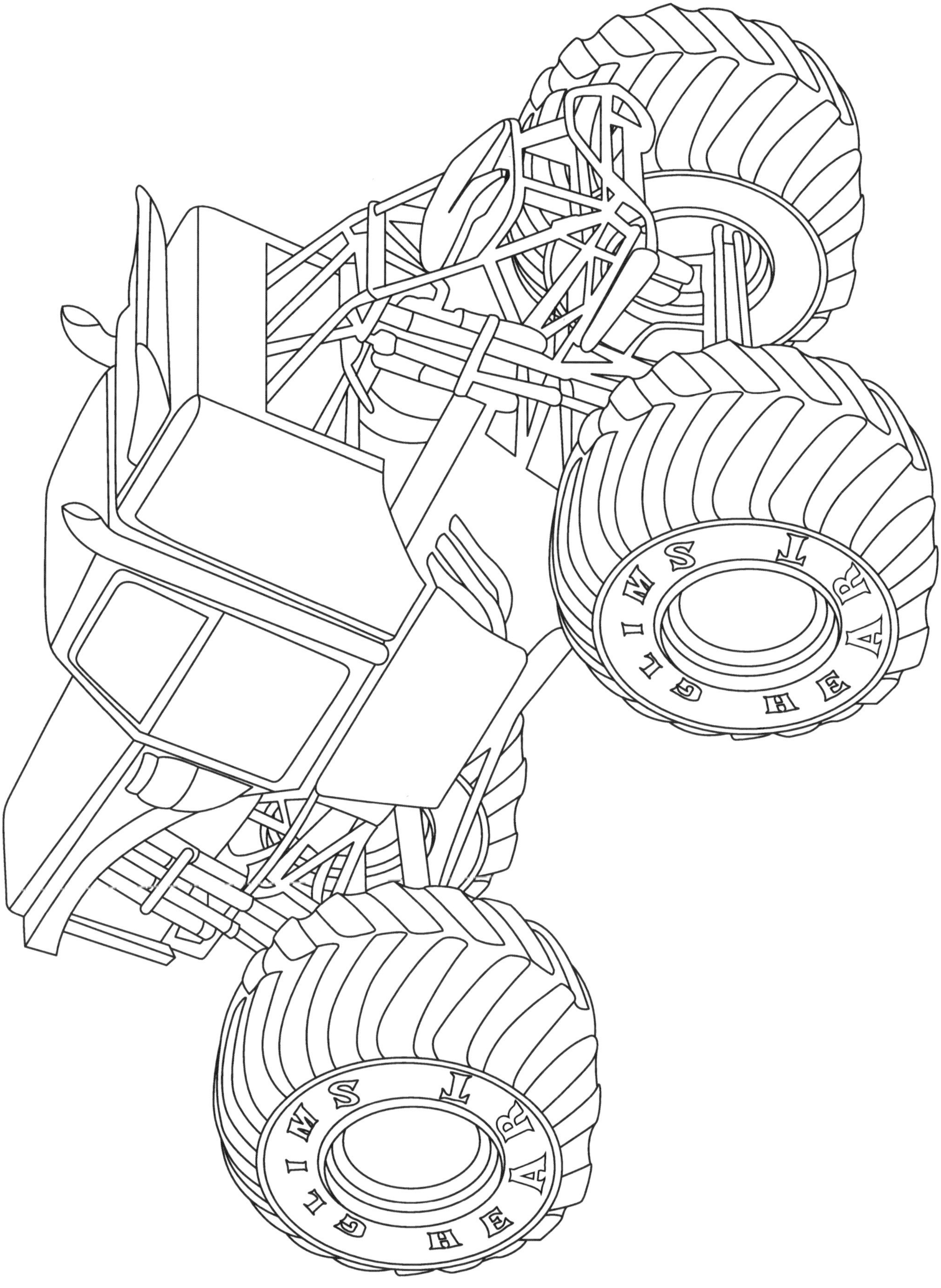

GUNS
HEART

GLIMS
HEART

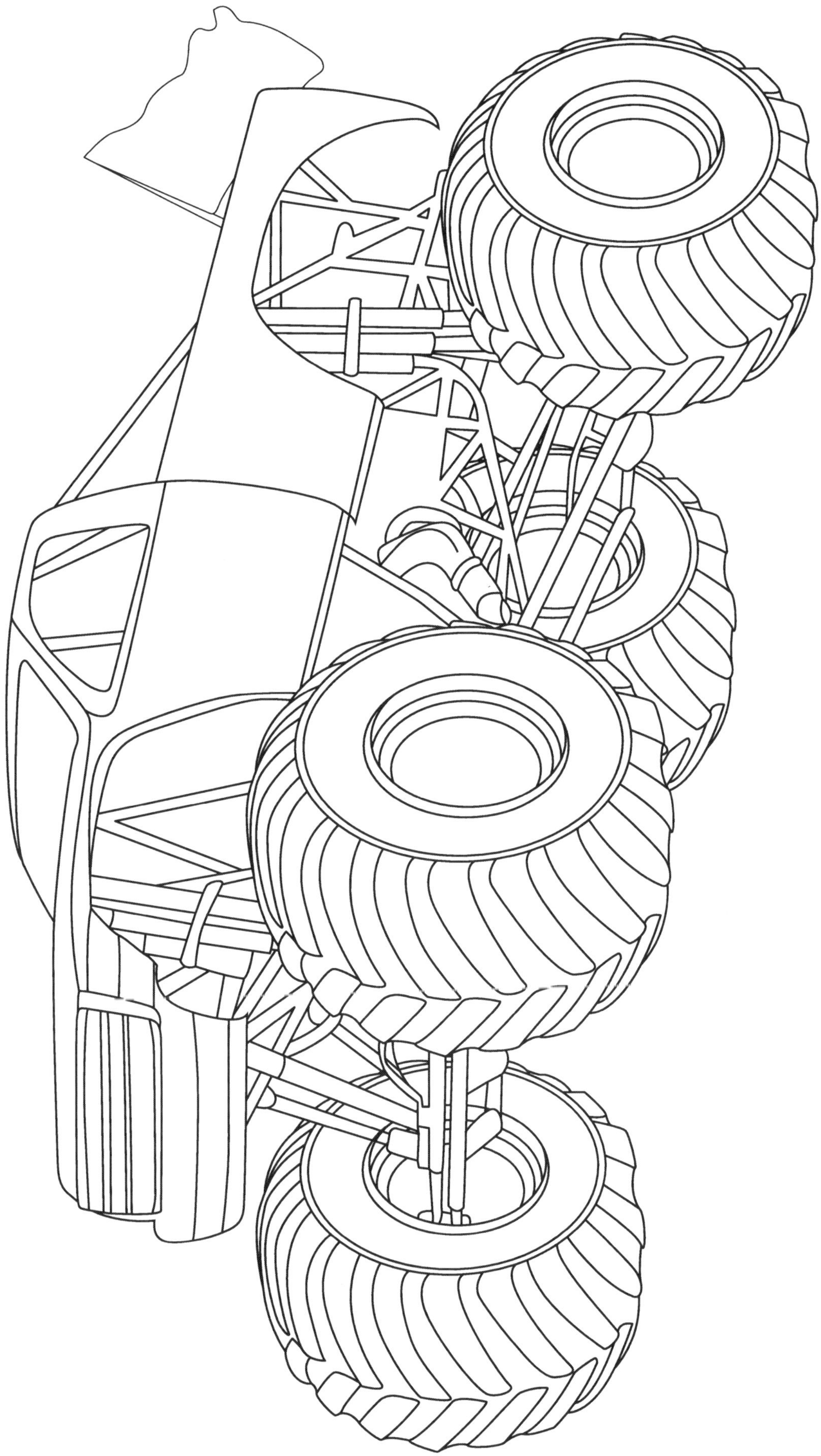

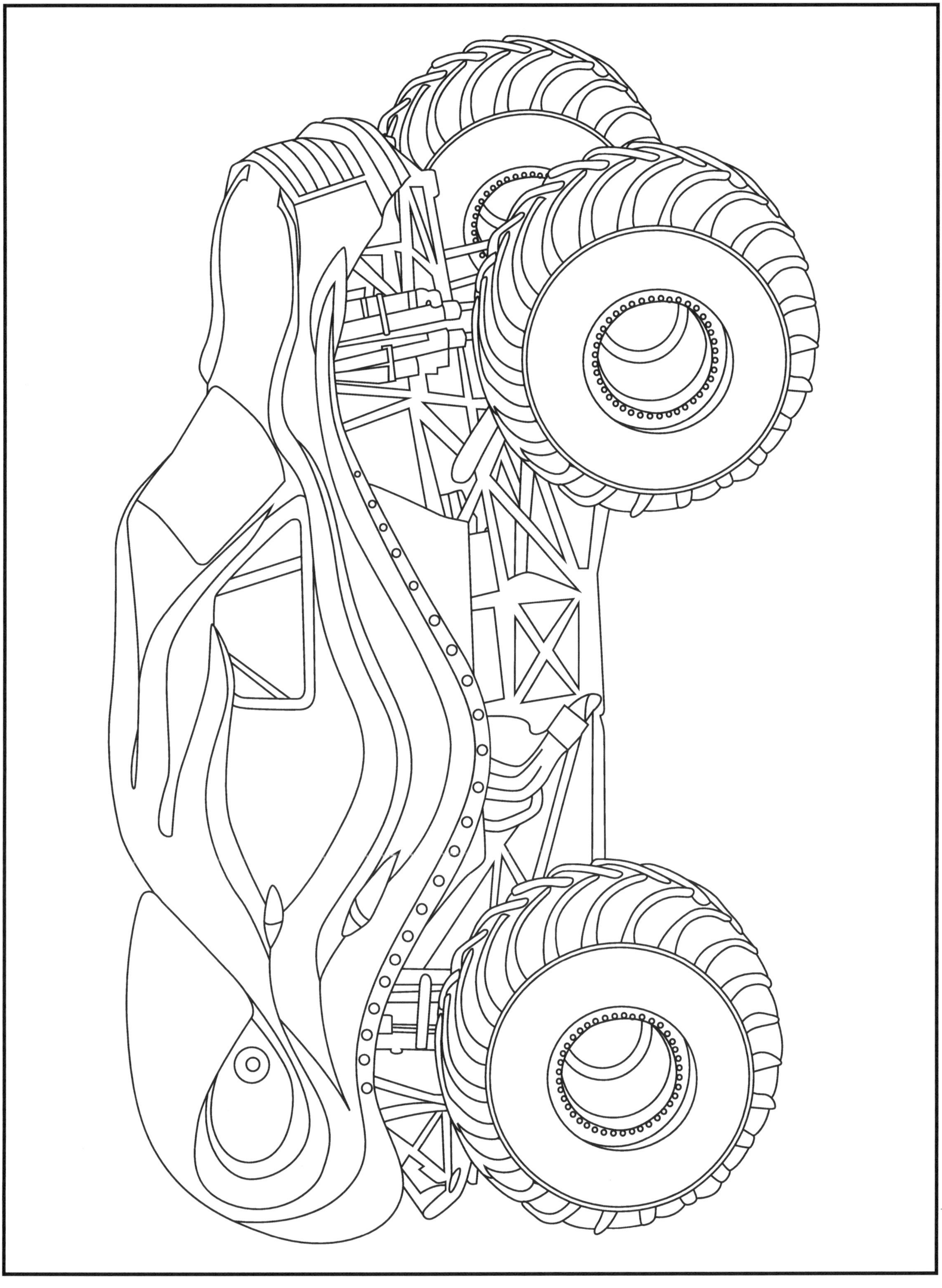

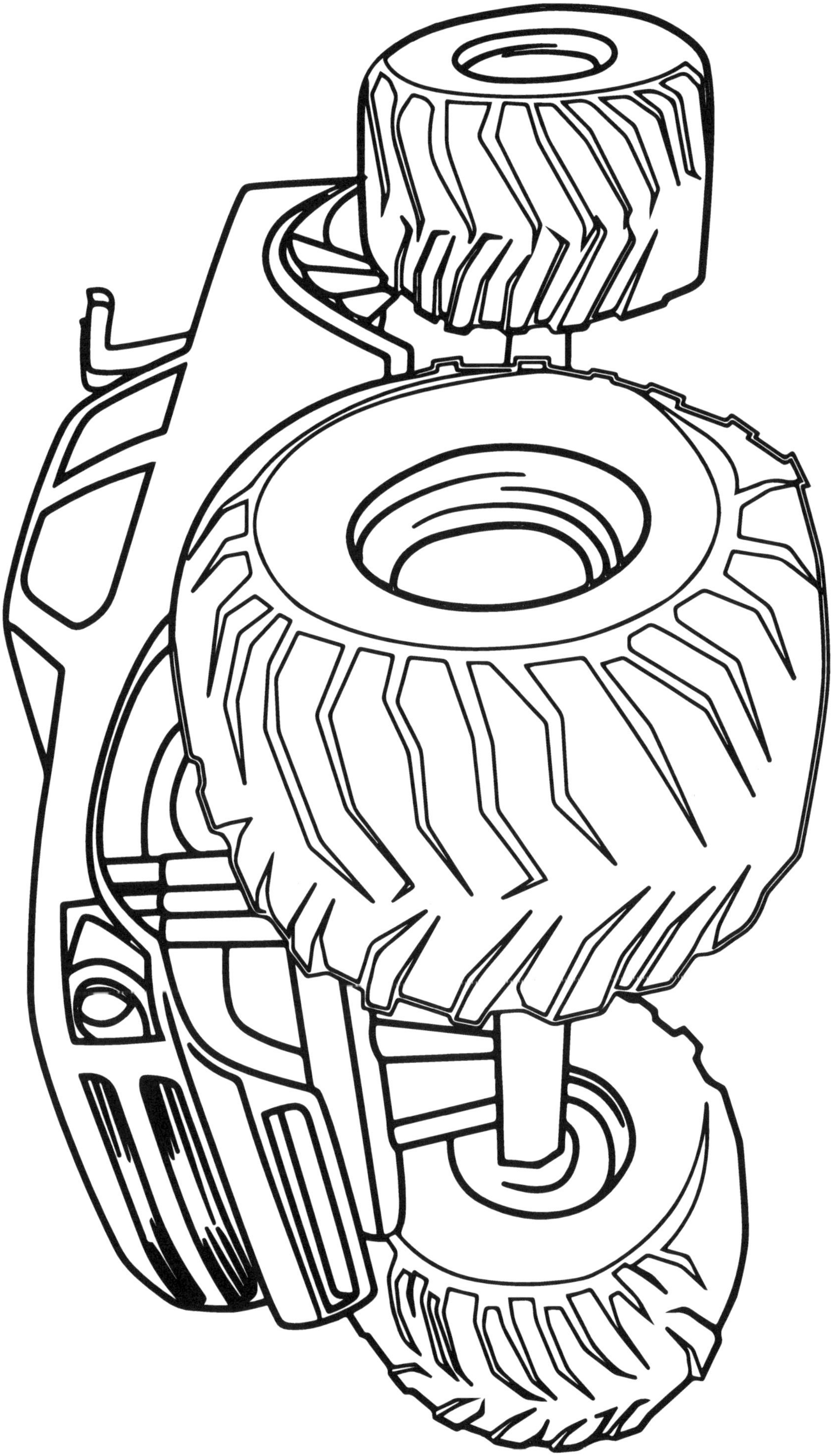

Made in United States
Troutdale, OR
11/24/2024

25257088R00035